Maurice Sendak

My Favorite Writer

Jennifer Hurtig

WEIGL PUBLISHERS INC.

Published by Weigl Publishers Inc.
350 5th Avenue, Suite 3304, PMB 6G
New York, NY 10118-0069

Web site: www.weigl.com

Library of Congress Cataloging-in-Publication Data

Hurtig, Jennifer.
  Maurice Sendak / Jennifer Hurtig.
    p. cm. -- (My favorite writer)
  Includes index.
  ISBN 1-59036-484-8 (lib. bdg. : alk. paper) -- ISBN 1-59036-485-6
(soft cover : alk. paper)
  1. Sendak, Maurice--Juvenile literature. 2. Authors, American--20th
century--Biography--Juvenile literature. 3. Children's stories--
Authorship--Juvenile literature. 4. Illustrators--United States--Biography-
-Juvenile literature. I. Title. II. Series.
  PS3569.E6Z7 2007
  741.6'42092--dc22
  [B]

                                        2006015267

Printed in the United States of America
1 2 3 4 5 6 7 8 9 0 09 08 07 06 05

Project Coordinator
Heather C. Hudak

Design
Terry Paulhus

All of the Internet URLs given in the book were valid at the time of
publication. However, due to the dynamic nature of the Internet, some
addresses may have changed, or sites may have ceased to exist since
publication. While the author and publisher regret any inconvenience this
may cause readers, no responsibility for any such changes can be accepted
by either the author or the publisher.

Contents

Maurice Sendak

MILESTONES

1928 Born June 10 in Brooklyn, New York

1946 Graduates from Lafayette High School

1947 His first drawings are published in *Atomics for the Millions*

1950 Meets Harper and Brothers children's book editor Ursula Nordstrom

1951 Illustrates his first children's book, *Wonderful Farm*

1956 Writes his first book, *Kenny's Window*

1963 *Where the Wild Things Are,* which Maurice wrote and illustrated, is published

1967 Suffers a heart attack; his dog Jennie dies

1975 His animated film, "Maurice Sendak's Really Rosie: Starring the Nutshell Kids," airs on CBS

1980 Opera of *Where the Wild Things Are* is produced

1982 Designs the musical production *Love for Three Oranges*

Maurice Sendak's talent was discovered when he was quite young. He always had an interest in reading and drawing. His books have illustrations of wild beasts, animals, and children. His **fantasy** tales take the reader into his childhood dreams and thoughts. When Maurice was growing up, he was often ill, and he spent a great deal of time in his bedroom. He often looked out the window. He made up stories about what was happening outdoors. Many of Maurice's stories are about young boys who go on adventures, like Maurice did in his imagination.

When Maurice was a teenager, he began trying to get his drawings published. He then landed a job at a toy store designing their window displays. His talent was discovered by an important editor. Soon, Maurice was illustrating books. By the time he was 34 years old, he had written seven books and illustrated 50. Maurice also has helped produce musicals. In addition, he wants to direct a movie based on his famous book *Where the Wild Things Are*.

Early Childhood

Maurice Sendak was born in Brooklyn, New York, on June 10, 1928. Maurice's parents, Philip and Sarah, moved from Poland to the United States before World War I. He has an older brother, Jack, and an older sister, Natalie. Maurice was nicknamed Murray.

As a child, Maurice watched many movies. He was fascinated by Mickey Mouse. He also was greatly influenced by Walt Disney's film *Fantasia*, which he saw when he was 12 years old. His father also told him bedtime stories. Maurice still remembers many of them.

Brooklyn is home to about 2.6 million people. It is one of five sections that make up New York City.

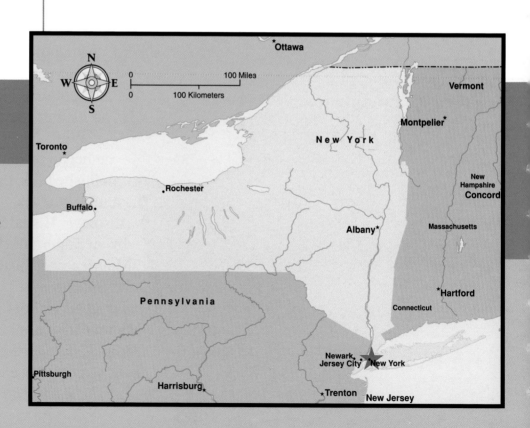

Maurice often stayed indoors because he suffered from illnesses. He had the measles. Then he caught pneumonia. Scarlet fever followed. Maurice observed what was happening outside of his bedroom window. Sometimes he drew pictures of what he saw. Maurice was not fond of school and did not excel at sports, but he liked to read. The first book Maurice owned was *The Prince and the Pauper* by Mark Twain. His sister, Natalie, gave him this book. After reading it, Maurice wanted to know how books were made. Maurice's brother, Jack, began to write stories and read them to his family. Maurice drew pictures to go with the stories and showed them as Jack read. When Maurice was 6 years old, he and Jack wrote a book called *They Were Inseparable*.

■ Maurice has enjoyed art projects all his life.

Growing Up

While in high school, Maurice began drawing for his school newspaper, the *Lafayette News*. The comic strip was called *Pinky Carrd*. Maurice also had a part-time job. He worked for All-American Comics, where he drew backgrounds for the *Mutt and Jeff* comic strip. Maurice's first job after he graduated from high school was with Timely Service, a window display company. He helped to build models for their window displays. He created life-size figures of Snow White and the Seven Dwarfs out of chicken wire and paper-mâché.

Maurice enjoyed working in Manhattan because he met many new people. He met an artist named Russell Hoban, who also worked at Timely Service. Russell was a painter. In time, Russell became a children's book author and illustrator. He and Maurice lived together for a while.

Maurice lived in Manhattan, which is a New York City borough. Manhattan is the most densely populated county in the United States.

8

Maurice eventually left this job and did not work for one summer. Along with his brother, Jack, he made wooden mechanical toys. Jack designed the toys, and Maurice carved and painted each one. The toys were inspired by stories and poems such as *Little Miss Muffet, Little Red Riding Hood, Hansel and Gretel, Aladdin's Lamp, Old Mother Hubbard,* and *Pinocchio*. The brothers took their toys to F.A.O. Schwartz, a toy store in New York City, to see if they could have them reproduced. They were told that it would be too expensive.

Maurice was inspired by children's stories, such as *Little Red Riding Hood*.

The window-display director thought that Maurice's work was very good. He offered him a job building window displays at F.A.O. Schwartz. Maurice accepted the offer and worked there for three years. At night, he attended painting and drawing classes at the New York Art Students League. He was inspired by the artwork in the children's books at F.A.O. Schwartz. Some of the artists were Walter Crane, George Cruikshank, and Hans Fischer.

■ F.A.O. Schwartz opened in New York City in 1870. The store on Fifth Avenue continues to be very popular and is one of the most famous buildings in the city.

Their cousin from the corn in blue;
Corn Marigold of golden hue.

"He was important for me because he communicated a sense of the enormous potential for motion, for aliveness in illustration. ... He was able to convey how much fun creating it could be," Maurice said of John Groth, one of his teachers at the Arts Students League.

Maurice enjoyed Walter Crane's art work.

Favorite Books

Maurice still has the first book he ever received. It is a copy of *The Prince and the Pauper* his sister gave him. Among his other favorites are *A Child's Garden of Verses* by Robert Louis Stevenson, adventure stories by authors such as Herman Melville, and the short story *The Luck of Roaring Camp (3)* by Bret Harte. Maurice loves books that allow him to use his imagination.

Learning the Craft

Maurice loved to read and to listen to his father's bedtime stories. His father's love of reading inspired Maurice to become a writer. Maurice enjoyed Mark Twain's books. His other favorite books included *A Child's Garden of Verses* by Robert Louis Stevenson and *Typee* and *2* by Herman Melville. Although Maurice did not enjoy school, he wanted to develop his talents. In high school, he practiced drawing. Many of Maurice's drawings are created using a technique called **crosshatching**.

Maurice was nervous about illustrating the first books he was assigned. He learned a great deal from Ruth Krauss, the author of one of the first books he illustrated. She was an experienced writer and taught him about publishing. Maurice's first illustrations were a **success**. He decided to leave the toy store and find more work illustrating books.

Maurice's books have **recurring themes**. The subjects of food, eating, and being eaten are in many of his books. Maurice thinks that eating is a very important part of a young child's life.

Mark Twain is a well-known U.S. author. Among his books are *The Adventures of Tom Sawyer, Huckleberry Finn,* and *The Celebrated Jumping Frog of Calaveras County.*

Practice helped Maurice improve his drawing skills.

To improve his work, Maurice listened to advice from people he knew. Some suggested books for him to read. Others told him to look at certain pieces of art. Maurice began to collect artwork that inspired him.

George Cruikshank, one of Maurice's favorite illustrators, drew pictures for *The Adventures of Oliver Twist* by Charles Dickens.

Getting Published

"Those beginning years revolved around my trips to the old Harper offices on Thirty-third Street and being fed books by Ursula, as well as encouraged with every drawing I did."
Maurice Sendak

Maurice's talent was discovered at a fairly young age. In high school, he made some drawings for a physics textbook called *Atomics for the Millions*. This was his first published work in a book. He was paid $100.

Maurice was only 22 years old when he had his next offer to illustrate a book. While he was working at F.A.O. Schwartz, he became friends with the store's book buyer, Frances Chrystie. She introduced Maurice to Ursula Nordstrom in 1950. Ursula was the children's book editor at the Harper and Brothers publishing house. Ursula saw Maurice's drawings. She offered him the chance to illustrate Marcel Aymé's book, *The Wonderful Farm*.

This was just the beginning of Maurice's successful career. Maurice drew the pictures for Ruth Krauss' *A Hole Is to Dig* in 1952. Ursula gave him more illustrating jobs and told him he should write his own stories.

In 1956, Maurice wrote his first book. The book was called *Kenny's Window*. Maurice drew all of the pictures for

The Publishing Process

Publishing companies receive hundreds of **manuscripts** from authors each year. Only a few manuscripts become books. Publishers must be sure that a manuscript will sell many copies. As a result, publishers reject most of the manuscripts they receive.

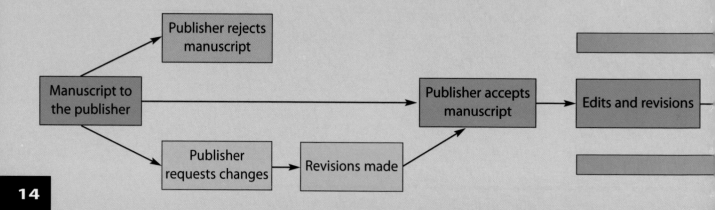

14

this book. The next year, *Very Far Away*, was published. Over the next 7 years, Maurice published one book almost every 2 years. He soon began receiving awards for his work.

Maurice moved out of his parents' house and found an apartment in Greenwood Village. Maurice was lonely, so he bought a Sealyham terrier. He named his dog Jennie, and she appears in many of his drawings. Maurice dedicated *Higglety, Pigglety, Pop!* to Jennie.

Maurice began trying new things. He started to **animate** books for movies and stage performances. His animated film, "Maurice Sendak's Really Rosie: Starring the Nutshell Kids," aired on television in 1975. Maurice, along with Carole King, a well-known singer, made a musical-play of the film called *Really Rosie*. By the time Maurice was 34, he had written seven books and illustrated 50. However, his drawings were not accepted by everyone because they included scary beasts. Maurice continued to draw and write in his own style.

Once a manuscript has been accepted, it goes through many stages before it is published. Often, authors change their work to follow an editor's suggestions. Once the book is published, some authors receive royalties. This is money based on book sales.

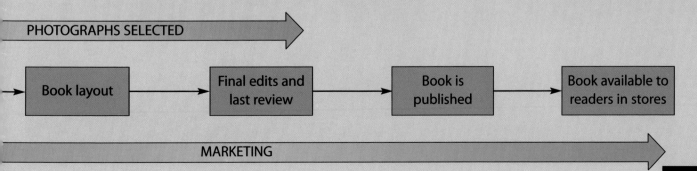

PHOTOGRAPHS SELECTED

Book layout → Final edits and last review → Book is published → Book available to readers in stores

MARKETING

Writer Today

■ Stage and musical productions of *Where the Wild Things Are* have been performed by theater groups around the world.

Maurice lives in Ridgefield, Connecticut. He has been ill a few times, so he does not travel much. Maurice has authored approximately 18 books and continues to write. He also has illustrated about 100 books.

Maurice is involved in the **performing arts**. He helps make television shows based on his books. He has designed musicals, such as *Love for Three Oranges* in 1985 and *A Selection* in 1999. Maurice has been the **artistic director** of The Night Kitchen, a national children's theater. He also wants to make a movie based on *Where the Wild Things Are*.

Maurice eats little during the week when he is writing and drawing. In the summer and autumn, he mainly eats vegetables he grows in his own garden. When he has visitors, however, Maurice reveals his inner child. He likes to share a meal of sandwiches and gooey chocolate desserts.

Maurice has never married. He loves children, but he has never had any of his own. Maurice has said he would not make a good parent because he spends too much time working. However, he has had quite a few pet dogs.

■ Maurice enjoys sharing his artwork with others.

Popular Books

Maurice's books are often based on his pets or on childhood dreams. Some of his books feature young children who go to faraway places on adventures, but then they return home. Maurice also draws the pictures in his books. He illustrates books for other authors, too.

AWARDS

Where the Wild Things Are

1964 Caldecott Medal

Where the Wild Things Are

Where the Wild Things Are is one of Maurice's most popular books. The story follows a boy named Max, who acts like a "wild thing." When he threatens to eat his mother, she sends him to this room without any dinner. Max's room turns into a jungle and an ocean. He sails away on a boat to a land that has wild creatures. The wild things crown Max as their king because he is able to control them. Max starts to feel homesick. Does he return home or stay with the wild things? Maurice drew all of the pictures in this book. The drawings are of large scary monsters, which are the "wild things."

In the Night Kitchen

In the Night Kitchen, a boy named Mickey has dreams of traveling through the Milky Way. One night, while he is dreaming, he falls from his bed into the night kitchen. The rest of the world is sleeping except for the bakers who make bread. In the kitchen, Mickey lands in a large bowl of cake batter. The bakers mistake Mickey for milk, so he jumps into a mound of bread dough. He molds the dough into an airplane and flies to the top of a huge milk bottle. Mickey dives into the bottle and scoops up a pitcher of milk for the bakers. He slides down the milk bottle and lands in his bed at home. Maurice named The Night Kitchen theater after this book.

The Nutshell Library

The Nutshell Library consists of four short books: *Alligators All Around, Chicken Soup with Rice, One Was Johnny,* and *Pierre*. All of these books are about children. *Alligators All Around* is an alphabet book illustrated by a family of three alligators that journey from A to Z. *One Was Johnny* features a young boy who lives by himself. He counts from one to ten and back again. In *Chicken Soup with Rice*, a boy travels through all of the months of the year. *Pierre* tells the story of a boy who once lived in the stomach of a hungry lion. In this tale, the boy is sent to live with humans.

AWARD

The Nutshell Library
1962 American Library Association Notable Book Award

Higglety Pigglety Pop!

In *Higglety Pigglety Pop!*, Jennie is a dog that has a large appetite and wants to eat everything. She devours plants, brown eggs, and vanilla pudding, but Jennie is not happy even though she lives a comfortable life. She goes on a journey to find something more for her life. Jennie finds out that she wants to be the leading actress at the World Mother Goose Theatre. Will Jennie live out her dream?

Outside Over There

In this story, a girl named Ida must watch her younger sister. While Ida is busy playing her horn, goblins kidnap her sister. Ida rushes to save her, and she climbs backward out of her window to "outside over there." Ida hears her father singing a song telling her to turn around. Once Ida turns around, she finds the goblins. She then plays her horn to **hypnotize** the goblins, which causes them to dance. Will Ida be able save her sister?

The Sign on Rosie's Door

Rosie was an imaginative girl in Maurice's neighborhood. She told stories to kids and performed for them, too. Maurice based *The Sign on Rosie's Door* on this real-life girl. Rosie is also featured in his animated television special "Really Rosie: Starring the Nutshell Kids." In this show, characters from the Nutshell Library books are Rosie's playmates.

The Sign on Rosie's Door is about a girl named Rosie who has a sign on her front door. The sign reads, "If you want to know a secret, knock three times." Kathy, Rosie's friend, knocks three times on the door, and Rosie tells her a secret. Rosie says that she is no longer Rosie. She is now Alinda, a singer. Kathy, along with Sal, Pudgy, and Dolly, has fun adventures with Alinda, especially during a Fourth of July celebration. At the end of this celebration, Alinda disappears, and Rosie returns. What does Rosie become afterward?

Very Far Away

This is the second book that Maurice wrote and illustrated. It is about a young boy named Martin, who has a new baby sibling. Suddenly, Martin does not get as much attention from his parents. He does not like this and goes searching "very far away" for someone to answer his questions. On his journey, Martin makes friends with a bird, a horse, and a cat. He soon runs home to his mother to see if she can answer more of his questions. Will his mother be there for him?

AWARDS
Outside Over There

1982 American Book Award

1970 Hans Christian Andersen International Medal for his work as a children's book illustrator

1983 Laura Ingalls Wilder Award for his contributions to children's literature

1996 National Medal of Arts for his body of work as illustrator and writer

2003 Astrid Lindgren Memorial Award for Literature

Creative Writing Tips

M aurice says that he has never spent less than two years on the text of his illustrated books. He begins to draw the pictures for his books only after the text is complete. He creates books this way so that the text has a great meaning even without any pictures. He then draws the pictures that match the text of the story. Here are some tips to think about as you write.

Research

Maurice observes what happens around him to come up with ideas for his books. For *Higglety, Pigglety, Pop!*, he watched his dog, Jennie, and the life changes she went through. He based this book on her and what she was like. Look at the things around you and in your home. Can you write a story about what you observe? Maybe you can draw pictures of what you see.

Maurice spends a great deal of time working on each book.

Read

Maurice started reading at a young age. He was greatly inspired by the books he read and the artwork he saw. The first book he owned, *The Prince and the Pauper*, made him want to know how books were made. He asked his friends what they read. Maurice read what they suggested to him. Ask your friends what books they read. You might enjoy reading those books. You can also go to a library and ask the librarian for reading suggestions.

Listen

As a child, Maurice was told bedtime stories by his father. The stories were often exciting and made Maurice use his imagination. Sometimes the stories were scary, too.

Maurice's father often shared **cliffhanger** stories. He would start the story on one night and continue the tale for many more nights. Maurice carefully listened to the tales. He could hardly wait to hear the next part of the story. Soon, he started making up his own stories.

Watch

Maurice watched many movies that inspired him to become an illustrator and a writer. Some of the movies that made a big **impact** on him include *Fantasia, King Kong,* and Charlie Chaplin films. Maurice also watched Mickey Mouse at a local theater.

Inspired to Write

Maurice says he is inspired to write by thinking of experiences from his childhood. For example, the wild thing characters in his most well-known book, *Where the Wild Things Are,* are based on his aunts and uncles. As a child, Maurice thought they were like toothy monsters trying to smother him with attention.

"With me, everything begins with writing. No pictures at all, you just shut the Polaroid off. ..."
Maurice Sendak

Writing a Biography Review

A biography is an account of an individual's life that is written by another person. Some people's lives are very interesting. In school, you may be asked to write a biography review. The first thing to do when writing a biography review is to decide whom you would like to learn about. Your school library or community library will have a large selection of biographies from which to choose.

Are you interested in an author, a sports figure, an inventor, a movie star, or a president? Finding the right book is your first task. Whether you choose to write your review on a biography of Maurice Sendak or another person, the task will be similar.

Begin your review by writing the title of the book, the author, and the person featured in the book. Then, start writing about the main events in the person's life. Include such things as where the person grew up and what his or her childhood was like.

You will want to add details about the person's adult life, such as whether he or she married or had children.

Next, write about what you think makes this person special. What kinds of experiences influenced this individual? For instance, did he or she grow up in unusual circumstances? Was the person determined to accomplish a goal? Include any details that surprised you.

A concept web is a useful research tool. Use the concept web on the right to begin researching your biography review.

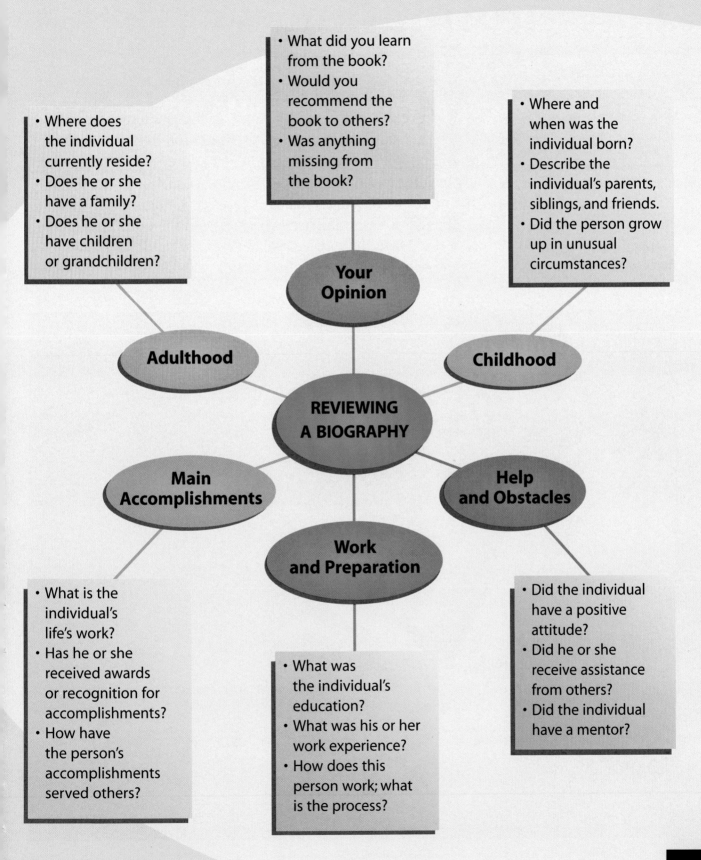

- What did you learn from the book?
- Would you recommend the book to others?
- Was anything missing from the book?

- Where does the individual currently reside?
- Does he or she have a family?
- Does he or she have children or grandchildren?

- Where and when was the individual born?
- Describe the individual's parents, siblings, and friends.
- Did the person grow up in unusual circumstances?

Your Opinion

Adulthood

Childhood

REVIEWING A BIOGRAPHY

Main Accomplishments

Help and Obstacles

Work and Preparation

- What is the individual's life's work?
- Has he or she received awards or recognition for accomplishments?
- How have the person's accomplishments served others?

- What was the individual's education?
- What was his or her work experience?
- How does this person work; what is the process?

- Did the individual have a positive attitude?
- Did he or she receive assistance from others?
- Did the individual have a mentor?

Fan Information

Maurice thinks that his young fans are his best **critics**. He says they are an honest audience. Maurice likes to get **feedback** on his work from young people. He wants to know if children enjoy or dislike his writing and illustrations. Many adult critics believed *Where the Wild Things Are* was too scary when it was first published. Children disagreed and made the book a huge success. More than 40 years later, *Where the Wild Things Are* is still a popular children's book.

Maurice makes time to meet with his fans.

Maurice continues to write and to help direct musicals for his fans to watch. He also writes and illustrates books. In addition, Maurice wants to make his stories into movies so his audience will have another form to enjoy his work. The Rosenbach Museum and Library in Philadelphia, Pennsylvania, has a display of many of his works. It also sells signed and rare books of his in its gift shop.

Maurice's creatures came to life during a performance of *Where the Wild Things Are.*

WEB LINKS

Maurice does not have his own website, but many other sites have information about him. For example, you can visit **www.barclayagency.com/sendak.html**.

You can find more information about Maurice's work on the Rosenbach Museum and Library website at **www.rosenbach.org/exhibitions/sendakgallery.html**.

Quiz

Q: What was the name of Maurice's high school newspaper?

1

A: *Lafayette News*

2

Q: Where was Maurice born?

A: *New York City*

3

Q: What was the name of his pet that was featured in some of his books?

A: *Jennie*

4

Q: What technique did he use for most of his drawings?

A: Crosshatching

5

Q: What was the first book Maurice owned?

A: The Prince and the Pauper by Mark Twain

6

Q: How many brothers and sisters did Maurice have?

A: One sister and one brother

7

Q: What year did "Maurice Sendak's Really Rosie: Starring the Nutshell Kids" air on television?

A: 1975

8

Q: How many children does Maurice have?

A: None

9

Q: What did Maurice do at F.A.O. Schwartz?

A: He designed window displays.

10

Q: What was the first book Maurice wrote?

A: Kenny's Window

Writing Terms

This glossary will introduce you to some of the main terms in the field of writing. Understanding these common writing terms will allow you to discuss your ideas about books and writing with others.

action: the moving events of a work of fiction

antagonist: the person in the story who opposes the main character

autobiography: a history of a person's life written by that person

biography: a written account of another person's life

character: a person in a story, poem, or play

climax: the most exciting moment or turning point in a story

episode: a short piece of action, or scene, in a story

fiction: stories about characters and events that are not real

foreshadow: hinting at something that is going to happen later in the book

imagery: a written description of a thing or idea that brings an image to mind

narrator: the speaker of the story who relates the events

nonfiction: writing that deals with real people and events

novel: published writing of considerable length that portrays characters within a story

plot: the order of events in a work of fiction

protagonist: the leading character of a story; often a likable character

resolution: the end of the story, when the conflict is settled

scene: a single episode in a story

setting: the place and time in which a work of fiction occurs

theme: an idea that runs throughout a work of fiction

Glossary

animate: to make a series of drawings that make it look as if a character or scene is actually moving

artistic director: the leader of a theater group who may do everything from hiring artists to picking the plays the group performs

cliffhanger: a suspenseful part of a story at the end of a chapter or scene

critics: people who offer their opinions on books, movies, or art

crosshatching: shading of drawings with two or more sets of intersecting parallel lines

fantasy: an invention of a creative imagination

feedback: returning information to the source

hypnotize: put into a trance

impact: the effect something has on someone

manuscripts: drafts of a story before it is published

performing arts: arts, such as dance, drama, or music, that are performed in front of an audience

recurring themes: common ideas that are featured more than once

success: to achieve something desired

Index

Photo Credits

Every reasonable effort has been made to trace ownership and to obtain permission to reprint copyright material. The publishers would be pleased to have any errors or omissions brought to their attention so that they may be corrected in subsequent printings.